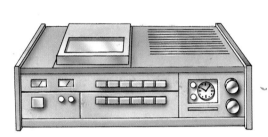

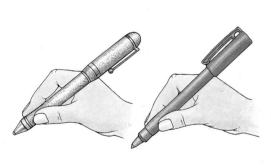
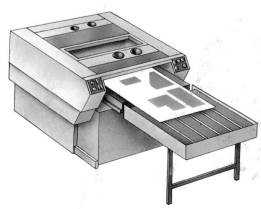
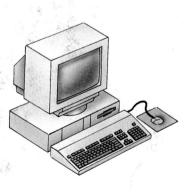

DOUNBY

PRIMARY SCHOOL

COMMUNICATION
THROUGH
TIME

CHRIS OXLADE

MACDONALD YOUNG BOOKS

First published in 1995 by Macdonald Young Books Ltd

© Macdonald Young Books Ltd 1995

Macdonald Young Books Ltd
Campus 400
Maylands Avenue
Hemel Hempstead
Herts HP2 7EZ

Design and typesetting: Roger Kohn Designs
Illustration: Ross Watton, The Garden Studio;
János Márffy; Alex Pang and Mike Taylor, Simon Girling
and Associates; Coral Mula; Roger Kohn
Commissioning editor: Debbie Fox
Editor: Caroline Wilson
Assistant editor: Jayne Booth
Picture Research: Val Mulcahy
Consultant: Neil Johannessen

Photo Acknowledgements
We are grateful to the following for permission
to reproduce photographs:
BT Pictures, page 42; BT Pictures (c. 1965), page 22;
British Library, page 12; Michael Holford, page 8;
NASA / Science Photo Library, page 34; Pains-Wessex
Limited, page 16, Science Photo Library, page 38
(Simon Fraser); Sygma / Patrick Forestier, page 28;
Zefa Pictures, page 18.

The publishers would like to thank the following for
their help: The BT Museum, Lancaster University,
Annie Walshe

Printed and bound in Portugal by Edições ASA.

ISBN 0 7500 1747 3

CONTENTS

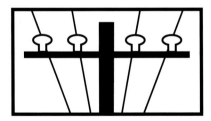

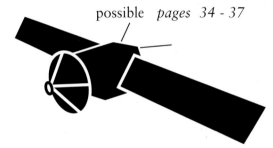

PENS AND PAPER

A SUMERIAN CLAY TABLET FROM 2100 BC
The Sumerians wrote down words as symbols and pictures. This sort of writing is called cuneiform writing. The marks were made by pressing a wedge-shaped nib into a soft clay tablet, which was baked afterwards to make the writing permanent.

You need three things to communicate with writing. The first is a way of writing down words which can be read by other people. The second and third are a material to write on, and a way of making marks on the material. People began making cave paintings nearly 50,000 years ago, but it was not until around

3500 BC that the first proper writing was developed. It was used by the Sumerians, who lived in what is now Iraq, and was carved on clay tablets. From around 3500 BC, the Egyptians used reeds, which grew along the banks of the Nile, to make both pens and paper (see far right). Later, they wrote on parchment, made from dried animal skin. The first paper, made from wood as ours is today, was invented in China in the second century BC.

EGYPTIAN HIEROGLYPHICS
The Egyptians developed their own system of writing using pictures and symbols. This was called hieroglyphics. Some pictures, or hieroglyphs, were carved or painted on walls. Others were written on papyrus with inks by specially trained scribes.

HOW PAPER WAS MADE

All paper is made by pressing together natural fibres into sheets and allowing them to dry. Papyrus was the first type of paper, made by the Egyptians from about 3500 BC onwards.

The reeds of the papyrus plant grew along the banks of the river Nile in Egypt, and it was one of the Egyptians' most important raw materials.

1 Paper-makers cut narrow strips from the pith found inside the reed stems.

2 They laid the strips across each other in two layers, horizontal and vertical, to make sheets.

3 The sheets were laid in a patchwork pattern, and then beaten flat, rolled smooth with a stone, and allowed to dry before being used.

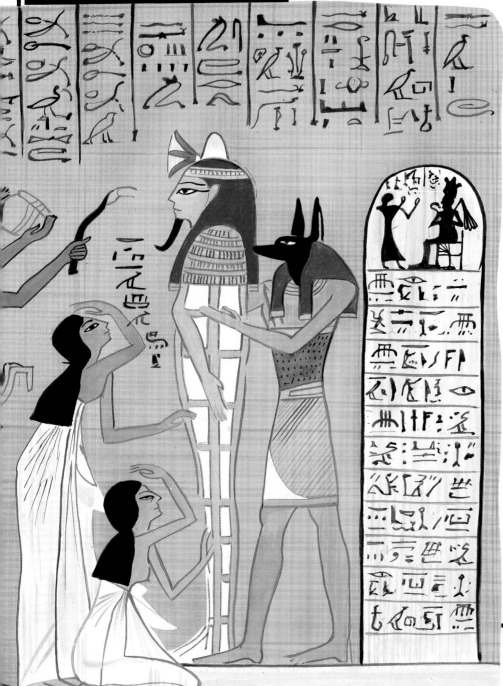

MODERN WRITING TOOLS

The most common writing tool today is the ball-point pen. It was invented in 1938 by Ladislao Biro. Modern manufacturing techniques make ball-point pen refills very cheap to produce, and many millions of disposable ball-point pens are sold around the world every day. Plastic-bodied pens with nylon writing tips, or felt-tip pens, are also popular.

The first typewriter was designed to help blind people write, and the machines became popular in the late nineteenth century. The 'QWERTY' arrangement of keys on modern typewriter keyboards – the name refers to the first letters in the top row of keys – was devised to slow down typists because fast typing jammed the mechanics of early machines. There are typewriters for most languages around the world. For languages without an alphabet, such as Chinese, typewriters may have thousands of characters to choose from.

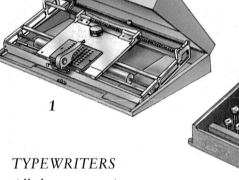

1

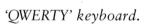

2

TYPEWRITERS
All these typewriters are constructed differently, but they all work by printing a letter and then moving the paper or print mechanism into place for the next letter.
1 A Hall typewriter built in 1890 by the Hall Type Writer Company of the USA. The typist chose the letters using a pointer.
2 A Sholes and Glidden typewriter from the 1870s. This was the first typewriter to have the standard

3

'QWERTY' keyboard.
3 An electronic wordprocessing typewriter from the 1990s. Text can be edited on the screen before it is printed.

PENS THROUGH THE AGES

The first pens were made from thin tubes found in nature, like reeds or feathers. They had to be regularly dipped in ink and wore out quickly. Modern pens work for many months before being refilled or thrown away.

500 BC
A quill was made from a goose feather with the end cut into a nib.

1884
The first successful fountain pen had to wait until non-clogging inks were developed.

MAKE A RE-USABLE CLAY TABLET

1 Cut a square wooden baseboard (about 20 cm x 20 cm) and glue four strips of wood along the edges to make a shallow tray.

2 Press lumps of modelling clay into the base. Smooth the clay into a flat layer with the back of a spoon.

3 Bend a thick paper clip into a V-shape and use it to cut out letters.

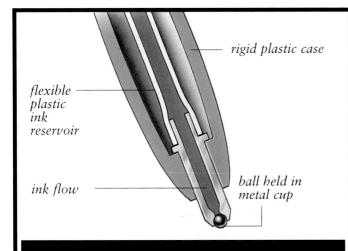

rigid plastic case

flexible plastic ink reservoir

ink flow

ball held in metal cup

THE BALL-POINT PEN

The ball-point pen is simple, but cleverly designed. As the pen moves over the paper, the ball turns, pulling down ink from the plastic reservoir behind.

1938-1990s
The ball-point pen is simple, reliable and disposable or refillable. Ball-points became widely available in the 1950s.

1960s-1990s
Felt-tip pens contain a felt pad with a tapered end which is saturated with ink that flows out on to the paper.

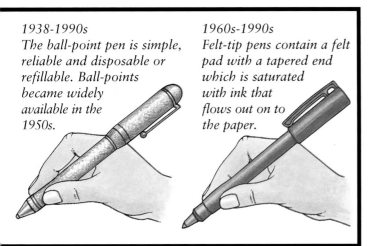

DELIVERING MESSAGES

Before the telegraph was invented (see pages 18-21), messages that were not passed by word of mouth had to be written down and delivered by hand. Messengers travelled on horseback for thousands of years until mechanical forms of transport like trains, ships and aircraft arrived.

Riders of the Pony Express delivered messages on horseback in the United States during the nineteenth century.

In the middle of the nineteenth century, new steam-powered ships made carrying mail overseas quicker and more reliable.

Air-mail services were introduced in the 1920s, and were a success in large countries like the United States.

PRINTING

Printing is a way of making many copies of a piece of text or a picture. The simplest method of printing is block printing, where a block of wood or stone is carved so that the letters to be printed are left standing out. The block is then covered in ink and pressed on to paper. This was first used in China over three thousand years ago.

The most important printing invention was called moveable type. Small blocks are engraved with letters or characters. Whole pages can then be printed by combining the letters, which are held together in a frame, and then pressing the frame on to paper. Moveable type was invented by Pi Sheng in China in about 1040, and by Johann Gutenburg in Germany in about 1440. Gutenburg also invented the printing press. Moveable type and printing presses made it possible to produce books much more quickly and cheaply than before. This was the first step in mass communication.

THE DIAMOND SUTRA
The Diamond Sutra is the earliest known printed book. It was probably printed in China in 868 AD. It was made by pressing carved wooden printing blocks on to a roll of paper by hand.

AN EARLY PRINTING PRESS
Johann Gutenburg developed the printing press from the type of press used for crushing grapes in wine-making. The type was inked using large pads and a sheet of paper was laid on top. You can see the large screw handle that turned and pressed the paper very firmly on to the inked type.

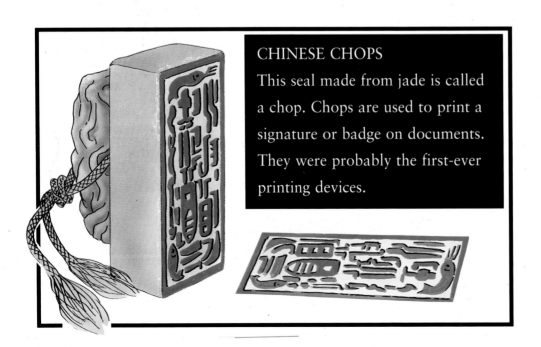

CHINESE CHOPS
This seal made from jade is called a chop. Chops are used to print a signature or badge on documents. They were probably the first-ever printing devices.

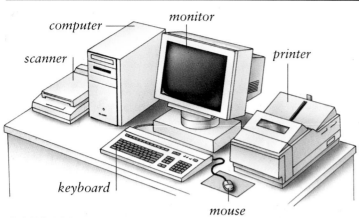

computer — monitor

scanner

printer

keyboard

mouse

LAYOUT

Text is typed in, or entered, at a keyboard. A scanner turns pictures into electronic form so that they can be shown on the screen. The layout is adjusted until the designer is happy with it.

MODERN PRINTING

Printed things – books, newspapers, magazines, leaflets and so on – are created using very high-tech equipment. But printing is just one of the stages in the production of a printed item. Before printing, the layout of the pages is designed on a computer. The pages appear on the computer screen just as they will appear in the final printed item, with type and pictures in their correct places. Text and pictures can be added or removed, made larger or smaller, moved around, or made a different colour or shade.

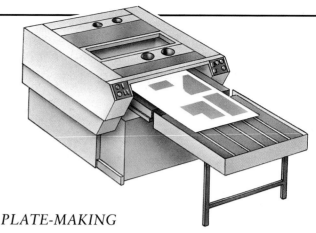

PLATE-MAKING

Printing plates are metal or plastic sheets with the pattern to be printed raised above the surface. To make one, text and pictures are copied photographically on to a flat plate. The plate is treated with chemicals that dissolve the parts that are not to be printed.

The computer can 're-run' text very quickly. For example, if an extra paragraph is added at the beginning of a novel, it takes just a few seconds for the computer to work out what text will be on all the following pages. The computer stores all the information about the pages ready for printing. The computerised pages are used to create printing plates, which are loaded on to the printing press. Most colour printing uses four printing plates and just four colours of ink. Thousands of colours can be printed by combining these four inks in different amounts.

ADVANCES IN TYPESETTING

Typesetting is the process of combining letters or characters of type into words, sentences, paragraphs or whole pages of text. Computers have revolutionised this process.

1040 AD
In China, Pi Sheng used baked clay blocks with carved characters on them. This was the first moveable type.

1440s
Johann Gutenburg developed metal moveable type. In 1448, someone gave him money to help him produce it.

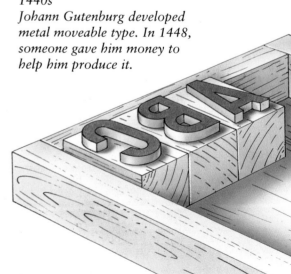

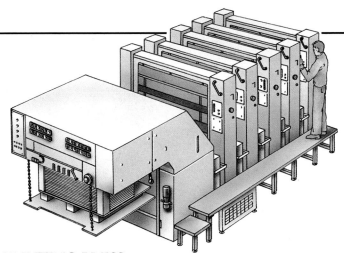

PRINTING PRESS

The printing plates are fixed around a cylinder in the press, and one sheet of paper is printed each time the cylinder revolves.

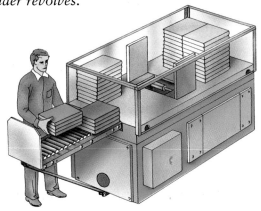

FINISHING

The printed sheets of paper are folded, put together in the right order, bound together by stapling or gluing, and trimmed to the correct size. This is all done by automatic machines.

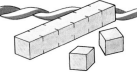

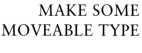

1 Cut several blocks of wood about 3 cm x 2 cm x 2 cm.

2 Form back-to-front letters with string and glue them on to the blocks.

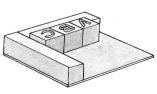

3 Glue two wooden strips to a card baseboard (about 30 cm x 30 cm) to make an L-shaped frame and put the blocks into the frame to make up words.

4 Use a paintbrush to cover the string letters with dark paint, or draw over them with a thick felt-tip pen.

5 Lay a sheet of paper over the type and press it down by rolling a bottle over it.

1930s
Hot metal typesetting meant that complete lines of type could be built by pouring molten metal into letter moulds.

1960s
Photocomposition is a photographic method of typesetting. The text is typed in at a keyboard.

1980s
Desk-top publishing allows typesetting and page design to be done on a personal computer.

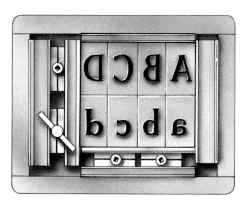

SIGNS

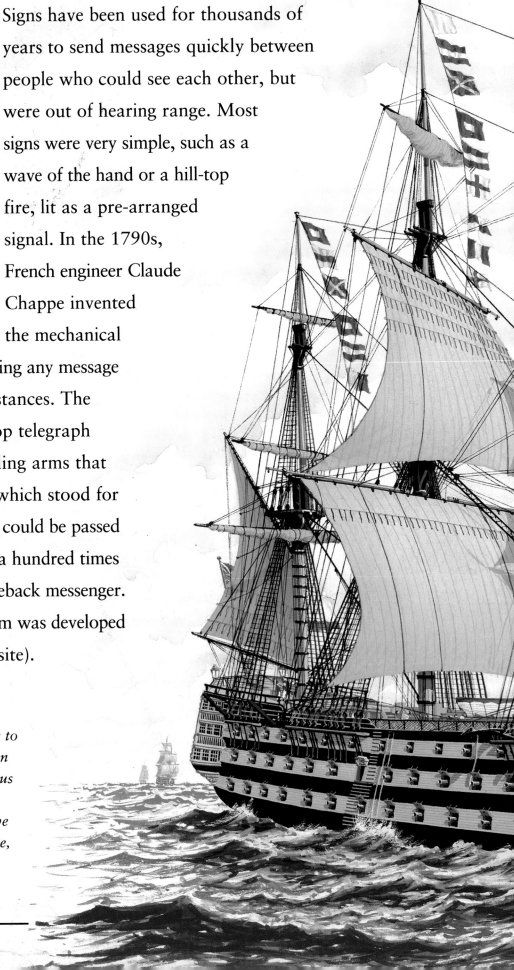

Signs have been used for thousands of years to send messages quickly between people who could see each other, but were out of hearing range. Most signs were very simple, such as a wave of the hand or a hill-top fire, lit as a pre-arranged signal. In the 1790s, French engineer Claude Chappe invented the mechanical semaphore system for sending any message quickly over very long distances. The system consisted of hill-top telegraph stations, each with signalling arms that were moved to positions which stood for different letters. Messages could be passed across the country almost a hundred times more quickly than by horseback messenger. A similar semaphore system was developed using two flags (see opposite).

AN EMERGENCY FLARE
Sailors always carry flares to use in case of emergency. They are like large fireworks, and give off a very bright light to attract attention.

Before radio was invented, code flags were the best way for ships to communicate at sea. Lord Nelson used code flags to send his famous message, 'England expects that every man will do his duty' at the Battle of Trafalgar in 1805. Here, HMS Victory *displays the first part of the message.*

HILL-TOP TELEGRAPH

By the 1850s, France had a network of over 500 optical telegraph stations. Messages were passed from hill-top to hill-top by moving the signalling arms into certain positions.

SENDING SEMAPHORE SIGNALS

Make two semaphore flags from light card and wooden sticks such as plant supports. Colour them as shown, and use the code to send messages to your friends.

20 cm
← 20 cm →

ELECTRIC COMMUNICATIONS

In the late eighteenth century, scientists slowly discovered the secrets of electricity and magnetism. They realised they could build a telegraph that used electricity to send messages along wires stretched between towns and cities. In all telegraphs, the person sending the message turned the electricity on and off, and this was detected by a receiving machine at the other end. The first telegraph was shown in 1809. To send a letter of a message, an electric current was sent along a wire used only for that letter. At the receiving station, the current caused small bubbles to form in a container of liquid. This told the person receiving the message which letter was being sent.

The machine used the newly invented battery.

TELEGRAPH WIRES
In the nineteenth century, railway companies in Europe and the USA built telegraph lines alongside their railways. Telegraph operators at railway stations could tell each other where the trains were.

Unfortunately each letter of the alphabet needed its own wire. Later machines used just a few wires, but the biggest step forwards was made in 1844, when American Samuel Morse demonstrated his single-wire telegraph. It used the now-famous Morse code of dots and dashes to represent different letters.

HOW A MORSE MACHINE WORKS

A Morse telegraph has two parts – a sender and a receiver. In Morse code, each letter is made up of a series of dots and dashes (for example, — · is 'a' and · · · is 's'). The operator presses a switch for short and long periods to send a sequence of dots and dashes. When the switch is closed, an electric current flows along the wire to the receiver. At the receiver, the current turning on and off makes a stylus draw a pattern of dots and dashes on a paper tape.

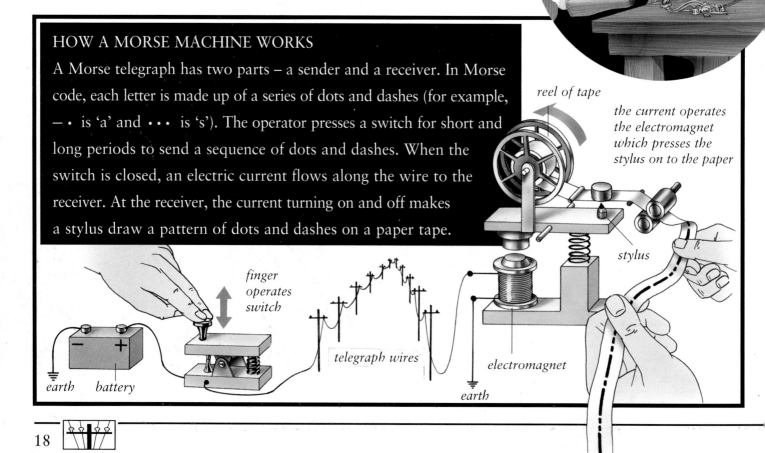

reel of tape

the current operates the electromagnet which presses the stylus on to the paper

stylus

finger operates switch

telegraph wires

electromagnet

earth   battery

earth

SAMUEL MORSE'S TELEGRAPH

Each telegraph operator had a 'key' for sending messages and a receiving machine that printed out incoming messages. A skilled operator could tap the sending key quickly enough to transmit up to ten words a minute.

COOKE AND WHEATSTONE TELEGRAPH

This telegraph was a two-wire machine which was used in Britain before Morse's less complicated system became popular. Twisting the handle on the sender made the needle on the receiver twitch from side to side. Different combinations of twitches indicated different letters.

MODERN TELEGRAPH COMMUNICATIONS

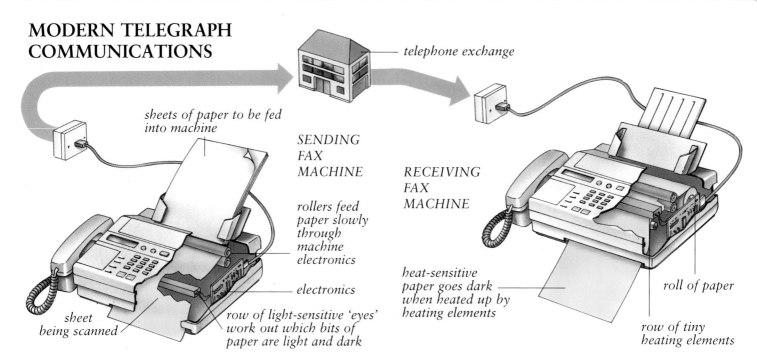

telephone exchange

sheets of paper to be fed into machine

SENDING FAX MACHINE

RECEIVING FAX MACHINE

rollers feed paper slowly through machine electronics

electronics

heat-sensitive paper goes dark when heated up by heating elements

roll of paper

sheet being scanned

row of light-sensitive 'eyes' work out which bits of paper are light and dark

row of tiny heating elements

BETTER TELEGRAPHS

Telegraph machines gradually became quicker and easier to use, with keyboards for typing messages, and machines to print them automatically. By the end of the nineteenth century, many countries had a telegraph office in every town. People could pay a small fee to have a message sent to another office, from where it was delivered by hand. Steamships laid telegraph cables under seas and oceans, allowing telegrams to be sent around the world.

WRITING BY TELEPHONE

As the telephone became more widely available around the turn of the century, people began to use it instead of sending telegrams. Business people, though, still wanted to send official messages by telegram. From the early 1930s, subscribers in Britain and the United States could use their own machines for sending written messages along telephone lines. The system was called telex (*tele*graph *ex*change). The message was typed in at the sender's keyboard and was immediately printed at the receiver's machine. Telegraph-type machines are now being replaced by fax machines and electronic mail (see page 40).

FAX

Fax is short for facsimile, which means an exact copy. A fax machine can send words and pictures because it sends an exact copy of a page. The first practical fax machine was built in the early 1900s, but it was not until electronics became cheap in the 1980s that fax machines became popular. A fax machine works by dividing each page it sends into thousands of tiny squares, and scanning it to work out whether each square is light or dark. The receiving fax machine prints tiny black squares on a blank sheet of paper where there were black squares on the original page.

ADVANCES IN TELEGRAPH MACHINES
Telegraph machines gradually became more automatic. This meant that operators did not need to code and decode Morse code.

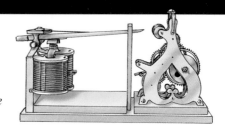

1844
Samuel Morse's single-wire telegraph machine used Morse code.

MAKE AN ELECTRIC TELEGRAPH

1 *Cut a piece of bell wire about 1 m long. Wind it around a steel nail to make an electromagnet. Bare the ends of the wire and tape the nail to a piece of stiff card.*

2 *Magnetise a needle by stroking it several times in the same direction with one end of a bar magnet.*

3 *Glue the magnetised needle to the end of a thin strip of paper (about 3 mm x 6 cm). Attach it to the card base with a piece of paper (about 2 cm x 4 cm) so that the needle points at the centre of the nail.*

4 *Using a small block of wood, make a switch with three drawing pins and a partly straightened paper clip, as shown.*

5 *Attach two 1.5 volt batteries (e.g. AA size) to the switch as shown, and connect the batteries and the switch to the needle indicator with two long pieces of wire.*

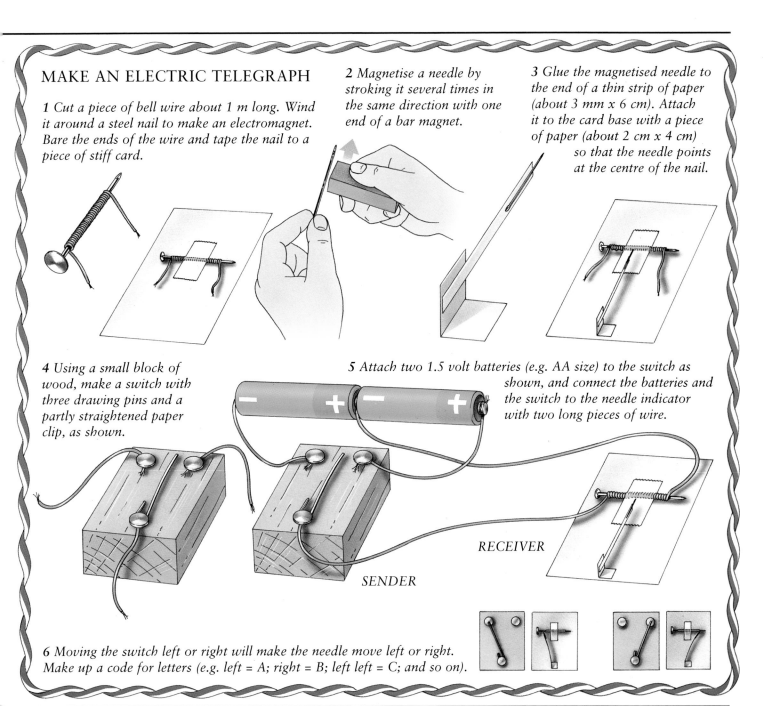

RECEIVER

SENDER

6 *Moving the switch left or right will make the needle move left or right. Make up a code for letters (e.g. left = A; right = B; left left = C; and so on).*

1875
The printing telegraph had a keyboard and could print messages automatically.

1932
Telex systems could send written messages to other people's telex machines.

1990s
Electronic mail, or e-mail (see page 40), is the modern equivalent of the telegraph.

THE TELEPHONE

Alexander Graham Bell was a Scotsman who emigrated to the United States, where he studied acoustics – the science of sound. In 1875 he was working on a telegraph system which would transmit several messages along a wire at the same time. By chance, Bell heard the sound of his assistant testing the apparatus in another room. He realised that the telegraph was transmitting sound, and began trying to build a telephone.

Bell's first telephone was quite simple. When you spoke into the mouthpiece, your voice was turned into a tiny electric current which changed in direction and strength. The current was like a code which represented the sound of your voice. This current flowed along a wire to the listener's earpiece, where it was turned back into sound. However, the telephone could manage little more than shouting distance because the signal was so weak. Bell tried different methods of making the signal from sound, but could not solve the problem. In 1878, American inventor Thomas Edison adopted the carbon microphone, which gave much stronger currents. The first telephone exchange was opened in 1878 in New Haven, United States, and within a few years, many cities had their own telephone systems. These were gradually linked together with long-distance telephone lines.

A NOVELTY TELEPHONE
From the 1940s and 1950s, when different plastics were developed, telephone receivers could be made in almost any shape. This Mickey Mouse telephone was introduced in the 1970s.

EARLY TELEPHONE EXCHANGES
Early telephone exchanges were very simple. There were no telephone numbers. To make a call, you pressed a simple button on your telephone which alerted the operator. The operator asked who you wanted to talk to, and plugged the two lines together.

A GOWER-BELL
TELEPHONE RECEIVER
This telephone was available
in the early 1880s, and was
one of many models with the
new carbon microphones.
Once fixed to the wall, it
stayed in good working order
with no need for adjustment.
This was a great
improvement on the Bell
receiver, which constantly
had to be adjusted at each
end. The Gower-Bell has the
mouthpiece on the top, with
the microphone hidden inside
the box. The earpiece is also
inside and the sound travels
along the two listening tubes
to the listener's ears. The
machine was large and heavy,
so it was placed inside a wall-
mounted box. Pressing the
button at the top indicated to
the operator that you wished
to make a call.

THE EDISON TELEPHONE
The American inventor, Thomas Edison,
developed an improved telephone using a
new carbon microphone. These microphones
were in use until the early 1990s. On this
version, you had to keep turning the handle on
the right to make the earpiece work.

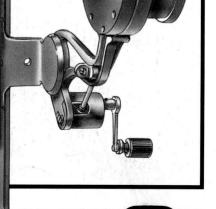

MODERN TELEPHONES

A modern telephone might look different to a telephone of fifty years ago, but it still does the same job. There is a mouthpiece, which converts your voice into an electrical signal, an earpiece, which converts electrical signals into sound, and a keypad or dial to tell the exchange the number you want. You can find out how telephone numbers work on page 26.

diaphragm vibrates, creating sound, when electrical signal goes through coil of wire

diaphragm

extendable aerial

earpiece (miniature loudspeaker)

keypad for dialling numbers

mouthpiece (microphone)

magnet

coil of wire

electronic circuits

thin metal discs vibrate when sound hits them

Most modern telephones have electronics that add extra features, such as memories to remember telephone numbers you use regularly. The low cost of electronics means that these sophisticated telephones are quite cheap to buy. The first mobile 'phones became available in the mid 1980s, when they cost about ten times as much as a normal 'phone. Today, they are almost as cheap.

MAKE A WORKING TELEPHONE

1 Using a sharp knife, cut two pieces from a cardboard tube, each about 7 cm long. Ask an adult to help you.

2 Stand the tubes on a sheet of paper, draw around them. Cut out circles 1 cm larger all round than the drawn circles, and make a series of cuts as shown.

3 Tape the paper circles to the ends of the tubes. Pierce a tiny hole in the centre of each circle.

4 Cut about 5 m of thread. Push one end through each hole and tie a knot to keep it in place.

5 Talk into one of the tubes while someone holds the other to their ear. You must keep the thread taut, or this will not work.

ADVANCES IN TELEPHONES

The most important advances in telephones have been automatic dialling and portability.

1881
The Gower-Bell telephone had two listening tubes and a central mouthpiece.

1905
Lifting the earpiece of this 'candlestick' telephone automatically called the exchange.

1920s
Once dials were introduced, telephones could be used with an automatic telephone exchange.

1990s
Most battery-powered mobile 'phones have a memory for storing the most useful telephone numbers.

MOBILE TELEPHONES

A mobile telephone, sometimes called a cellphone, is a combination of a telephone and a walkie-talkie radio. The mouthpiece and earpiece change the sound of your voice into an electrical signal and back again, just like a normal telephone. But instead of the signal going along a wire to the telephone exchange, it travels through the air as a radio signal. The radio signal goes from your telephone's aerial to an aerial which is connected to a telephone exchange (see page 26). The voice of a person talking back to you goes to the telephone exchange as an electrical signal, is changed to a radio signal at the transmitter, is detected by your mobile 'phone, and converted back to sound. There are many receiving and transmitting stations dotted about the countryside. Each one handles calls to and from mobile telephones that are in a certain area, called a cell.

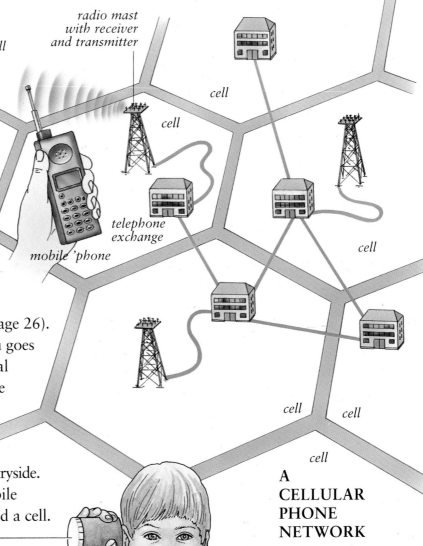

radio mast with receiver and transmitter

cell

cell

cell

telephone exchange

mobile 'phone

cell

cell

cell

cell

cell

A CELLULAR PHONE NETWORK

ELECTRONIC EXCHANGES

All the telephone lines in one area are connected to a local telephone exchange. At the exchange, each line can be connected to a line to another local telephone, or to a line to another exchange. In early exchanges, an operator connected lines by plugging them together. Automatic exchanges can tell what number is being dialled and make the connection automatically. From the turn of the century, these new exchanges used switches controlled by electromagnets. Modern electronic exchanges are controlled by computer. They have no moving parts, so they are smaller, cheaper and more reliable. The computer makes it easier for the telephone company to record calls and change telephone numbers, and it makes connections much quicker. Each telephone is connected to the exchange by its own line, but lines between exchanges may carry thousands of calls at once.

OPTICAL FIBRES

Originally, all telephone lines were made with copper wires. However, most trunk lines are now optical-fibre cables, and contain anything up to 12 fibres. An optical fibre is a thin thread of glass with a clear plastic cladding. Light shone into one end of the fibre travels along it, bouncing off the inside surface.

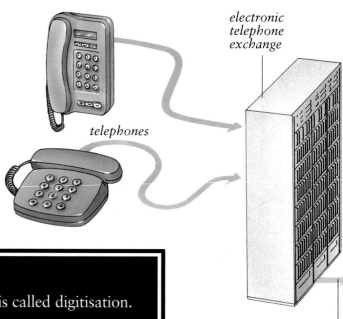

electronic telephone exchange

telephones

optical-fibre trunk line

DIGITISATION

The most recent development in telephone systems is called digitisation. In a digital system, a signal is turned into a simple code called binary, where the current is either on or off, instead of changing in strength. It gives much better sound quality, and many more signals can be sent along a single cable or optical fibre at the same time. Most telephone calls are digitised as they travel between telephone exchanges. But between the exchange and our telephones most still use the normal system.

The normal system sends a sound wave (your voice) as an electrical current which changes in strength.

soft sound wave

loud sound wave

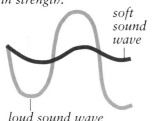

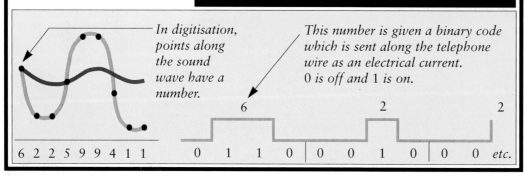

In digitisation, points along the sound wave have a number.

This number is given a binary code which is sent along the telephone wire as an electrical current. 0 is off and 1 is on.

| 6 | | | 2 | | 2 |

6 2 2 5 9 9 4 1 1   0 1 1 0 0 0 1 0 0 0 *etc.*

1878
The first human-operated exchange had just 21 lines. The first automatic exchange was devised in 1889.

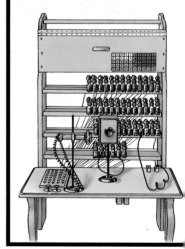

At the telephone exchange, electrical signals are changed into pulses of light, which flash along the fibre to the next exchange, where they are changed back to electrical signals. A single hair-thin fibre can carry thousands of calls at once, and a whole cable can carry up to 40,000! Calls sent along optical fibres do not suffer from electrical interference, and so are much clearer.

AN OPTICAL FIBRE

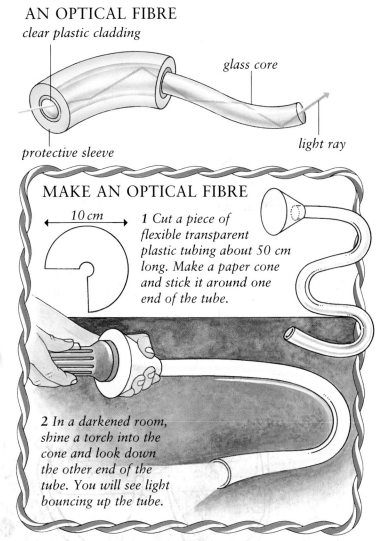

clear plastic cladding

glass core

protective sleeve

light ray

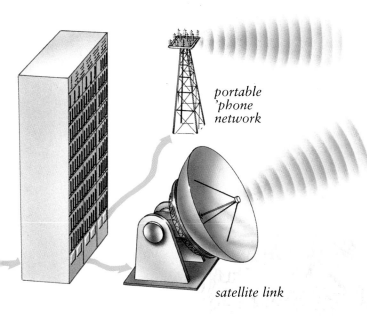

portable 'phone network

satellite link

MAKE AN OPTICAL FIBRE

10 cm

1 Cut a piece of flexible transparent plastic tubing about 50 cm long. Make a paper cone and stick it around one end of the tube.

2 In a darkened room, shine a torch into the cone and look down the other end of the tube. You will see light bouncing up the tube.

ADVANCES IN TELEPHONE SYSTEMS

Improvements in telephone exchanges, telephone cables and other telephone links make telephone communications cheaper and more reliable all the time.

1960s-1990s
Electronic telephone exchanges are smaller and more reliable than manual exchanges.

1965
The Earlybird satellite (Intelsat 1) carried up to 240 'phone calls across the Atlantic.

1956
An underwater, transatlantic telephone line was laid between Europe and the United States. It could handle 36 'phone calls.

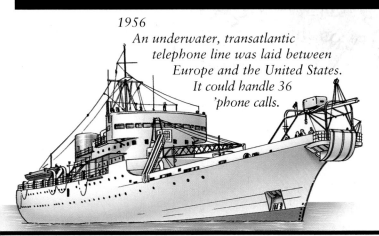

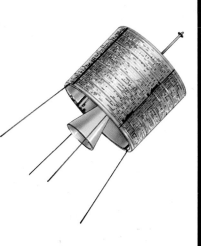

TELEVISION NEWS
Thanks to television, news programmes can bring events from around the world to our homes as they happen.

AN EKCO RADIO RECEIVER FROM 1938
Radio broadcasting started in the early 1920s, and by 1925 there were 600 radio stations around the world. Radios like this one were a focal point of many homes, just as televisions are today.

In 1888, the German physicist, Heinrich Hertz, carried out experiments which showed that radio waves exist. An Italian, Guglielmo Marconi, heard about Hertz's work and began to experiment with sending messages using radio waves. In 1895, Marconi successfully sent Morse code signals from a transmitter to a receiver over two kilometres away, and in 1901 he sent signals across the Atlantic. Radio was soon being used at sea. For the first time, ships could communicate when they were out of sight of each other. In the early 1900s, Reginald Fessenden, a Canadian pioneer of radio, developed a way of sending speech and other sounds by radio, rather than just simple dots and dashes.

The first successful demonstration of television was made in 1926 by Scottish inventor John Logie Baird. He succeeded in sending signals from a camera to a receiver via radio waves. However, his system used large and heavy mechanical equipment at each end, and eventually people developed electronic cameras and receivers instead.

MAKE SOME RADIO WAVES

To make radio waves, you have to send a changing electric current through an antenna. You can make your own simple antenna with a battery and some wire.

1 *Cut a piece of bell wire about 2 m long and bare the ends. Attach one end to the top of a 1.5 volt battery with sticky tape.*

2 *Turn on a transistor radio, and switch it to AM (or medium wave). Tune the radio so that you hear hissing rather than a radio station.*

3 *Hold the wire near the radio and stroke the remaining end across the other battery terminal (on the bottom of the battery). The changing current will create radio waves which the radio will pick up – you will hear a crackling noise!*

A TELEVISION SET OF 1936

Sets like this received some of the very first television broadcasts, which started in Britain in 1936, and in the United States in 1939. The glass tube which formed the picture inside an early television was long and thin. This meant the cabinet had to be large, while the screen was only around 18 cm wide. A set cost about £100 – several months' salary for most people at the time. Television pictures were in black and white, and there was only one channel, which broadcast for just a few hours each day. The programmes were news bulletins, cartoons and a few entertainment shows.

SENDING RADIO SIGNALS

At a radio station, the sound waves of a presenter's voice are turned into electrical signals by a microphone. Music can be added as electrical signals from CD players and tape players. The electrical signal is then used to change the shape of a radio signal called a carrier signal. A carrier signal is a bit like a carrier pigeon. It doesn't change the message, but simply carries it from the transmitter to the receiver. Radio waves spread out in all directions from the transmitter's aerial. Different radio stations use carrier waves with different frequencies (see page 43) so that radio receivers can tell one station from another. Walkie-talkie radios and portable telephones use a similar system to send radio signals.

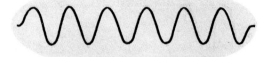

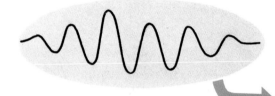

electrical signal used to change shape of carrier signal

sent from transmitter

this is called amplitude modulation

shaped carrier signal sent to transmitter

microphone converts sound waves into electric current of changing strength (called an electrical signal)

sound waves

AM AND FM
Most radios can receive both AM and FM signals. AM stands for amplitude modulation and FM stands for frequency modulation. They are different ways of transmitting a signal on a

DEVELOPMENTS IN RADIO RECEIVERS
Advances in electronics have allowed radio receivers to become smaller and easier to tune.

1910s
With a simple 'crystal' radio receiver you had to use headphones for listening.

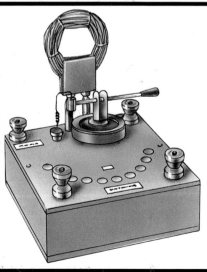

1920s
These receivers used valves to amplify (make bigger) signals to work a loudspeaker.

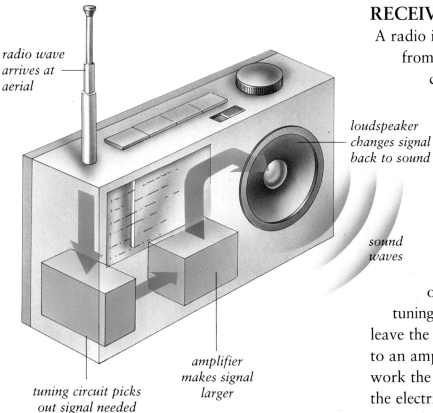

radio wave arrives at aerial

loudspeaker changes signal back to sound

sound waves

tuning circuit picks out signal needed

amplifier makes signal larger

RECEIVING RADIO SIGNALS

A radio is designed to collect the radio signal from the station required, take away the carrier wave to leave the original electrical signal, and reproduce the sound. The inside of a radio looks complicated, but you can think of it in four basic sections: aerial, tuning circuit, amplifier and loudspeaker. Radio waves from many different transmitters enter the aerial, causing tiny electric signals in it. The radio's tuning circuit picks out carrier waves of the frequency you select by turning the tuning knob, and removes the carrier wave to leave the original signal. The signal is passed on to an amplifier, which makes it strong enough to work the loudspeaker. The loudspeaker turns the electrical signal back into sound.

carrier wave. FM gives clearer sound but you need more power to send the signal and more complicated transmitting and receiving equipment to hear it.

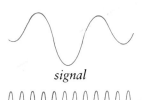

signal

carrier wave

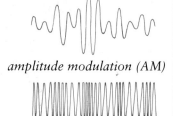

amplitude modulation (AM)

frequency modulation (FM)

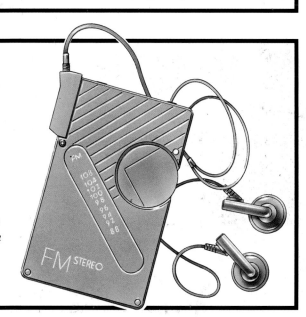

1954
Transistorised radios used the newly invented transistor instead of valves.

1980s
FM and AM radios are smaller and can receive broadcasts in stereo sound.

HOW TELEVISION WORKS

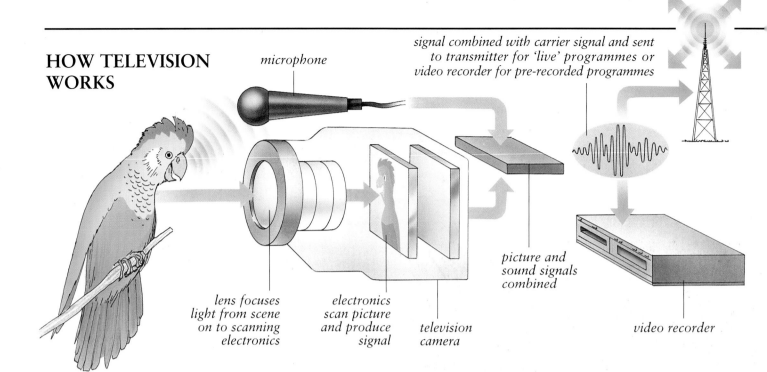

microphone

signal combined with carrier signal and sent to transmitter for 'live' programmes or video recorder for pre-recorded programmes

lens focuses light from scene on to scanning electronics

electronics scan picture and produce signal

television camera

picture and sound signals combined

video recorder

Television works in a similar way to radio. Pictures and sounds are converted to electrical signals, which are transmitted as radio waves. A television receiver detects the signals and turns them back into pictures and sounds.

A television camera divides a picture into hundreds of horizontal lines and electronically scans each line, working out the brightness and colour of the picture along the line. The information for the whole picture is sent line by line as an electrical signal. The scanning process is repeated 25 or 30 times per second. The signal is added to a carrier signal and sent to a transmitter.

A television receiver (television set) collects radio signals from the transmitter. Electronic circuits pick out the signal for the station needed and take away the carrier signal to leave the original signal. The signal is used to control three beams of tiny particles called electrons, one for each of the colours red, blue and green. The beams scan the back of the screen, making it glow, to reproduce the picture.

Video cameras do the same job as television cameras, but the pictures are not quite as detailed. Most use a single, light-sensitive microchip to convert the picture into an electrical signal.

THE HISTORY OF TELEVISION

Television today is basically the same as it was in the 1930s, but the pictures and sound are much clearer and in colour. We can also record them on videotape when we want to. Colour broadcasting started in the 1960s in the UK.

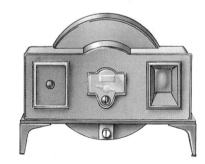

1926 Scotsman John Logie Baird invented the first basic, mechanical television system.

1930s Commercial television sets were available to receive early television broadcasts.

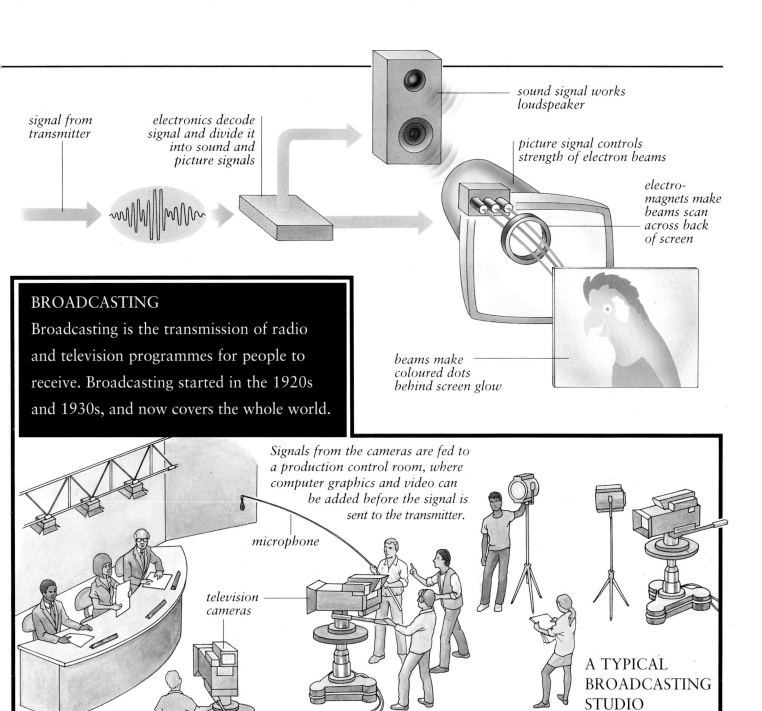

signal from transmitter

electronics decode signal and divide it into sound and picture signals

sound signal works loudspeaker

picture signal controls strength of electron beams

electro-magnets make beams scan across back of screen

beams make coloured dots behind screen glow

BROADCASTING

Broadcasting is the transmission of radio and television programmes for people to receive. Broadcasting started in the 1920s and 1930s, and now covers the whole world.

Signals from the cameras are fed to a production control room, where computer graphics and video can be added before the signal is sent to the transmitter.

microphone

television cameras

A TYPICAL BROADCASTING STUDIO

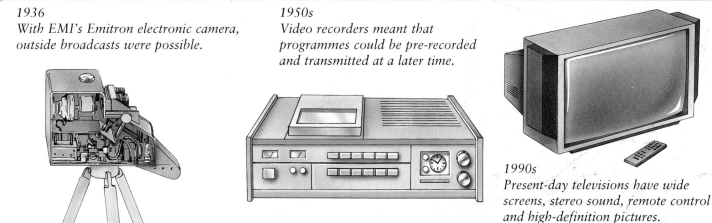

1936
With EMI's Emitron electronic camera, outside broadcasts were possible.

1950s
Video recorders meant that programmes could be pre-recorded and transmitted at a later time.

1990s
Present-day televisions have wide screens, stereo sound, remote control and high-definition pictures.

SATELLITE COMMUNICATIONS

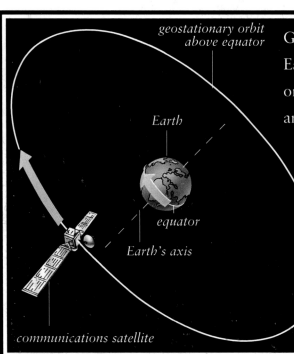

WESTAR V1 SATELLITE
A crew member of the Space Shuttle Discovery *retrieving the satellite. Astronauts can launch these satellites out from their own shuttle's 'low' orbit, and can also carry out repairs on satellites.*

In 1945, the famous science-fiction writer, Arthur C Clark, put forward the idea of communications satellites. He said that radio signals could be beamed from a transmitter up to a satellite, and back down to a receiver thousands of kilometres from the transmitter. But in 1945 there were no rockets powerful enough to travel out of the Earth's atmosphere and into space. It was not until 1960 that an experimental communications satellite called *Echo 1* was launched. It was a ball, 30 metres across, coated in aluminium to reflect radio signals. *Echo 1* worked, but by the time the signals reached Earth again, they were extremely weak. The *Telstar* satellite, launched in 1962, was a great improvement. It carried electronics that could boost signals before sending them back to Earth. It communicated with transmitting and receiving stations in the United States and Europe, and relayed the first live television pictures across the Atlantic. It could also relay up to 60 telephone calls.

geostationary orbit above equator

Earth

equator

Earth's axis

communications satellite

GEOSTATIONARY ORBITS
Early communications satellites travelled in low orbits, close to the Earth, which meant they went around the Earth once every few hours. They were only in the right place for sending signals for a few minutes during each orbit, which was no good for communications. Most communications satellites travel in a geo-stationary orbit, 32,800 kilometres above the Earth – about one-tenth of the distance to the moon. Here, they orbit at the same speed as the Earth spins on its axis, so that they stay above the same spot on the Earth.

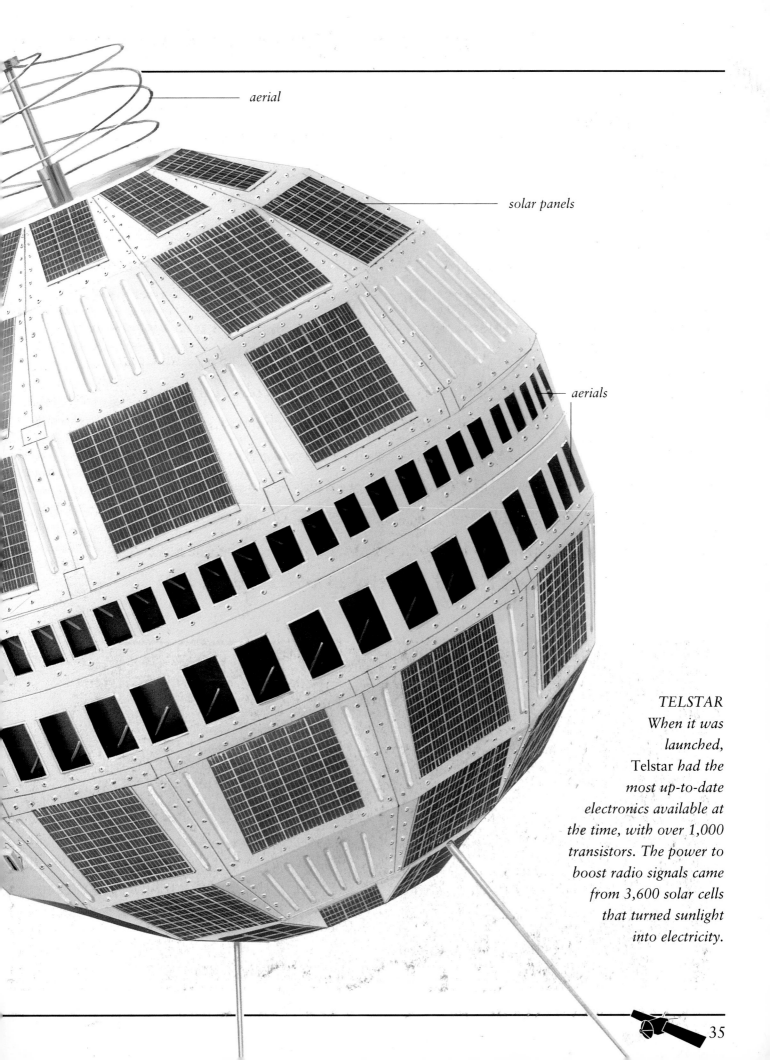

aerial

solar panels

aerials

TELSTAR
When it was
launched,
Telstar *had the
most up-to-date
electronics available at
the time, with over 1,000
transistors. The power to
boost radio signals came
from 3,600 solar cells
that turned sunlight
into electricity.*

HOW A SATELLITE COMMUNICATES

The Astra satellite system consists of several satellites in geostationary orbits. The system relays television and radio signals directly to millions of homes throughout Europe. The newest Astra satellites can relay digital signals.

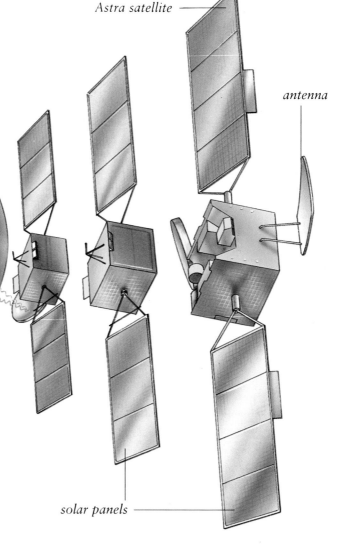

Astra satellite

antenna

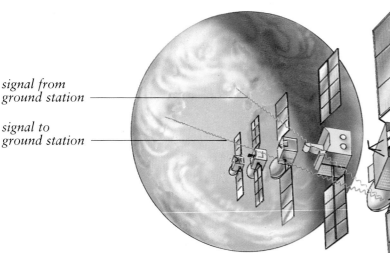

signal from
ground station

signal to
ground station

solar panels

Today, there are dozens of communications satellites orbiting above the Earth. They relay information from many sources – telephone calls, television stations, radio stations, telex signals and computer information. A modern communications satellite can handle tens of thousands of telephone calls and several television channels at the same time. It works completely automatically. The power to operate the on-board electronic circuits comes from solar panels, which turn sunlight into electricity. The satellite also has batteries to power it when it passes into the Earth's shadow. Tiny rocket motors can be fired if it drifts out of its correct position. Antennae aimed at the Earth receive and transmit signals. Signals are sent to satellites from satellite dishes at ground stations. A dish makes a narrow beam of signals which is aimed at the satellite. Other dishes collect signals coming down from satellites. The bigger the collecting dish, the better it picks up signals.

ADVANCES IN SATELLITES

Advances in electronics and rocket technology in the last 40 years have made satellites more powerful, more reliable and easier to launch and repair.

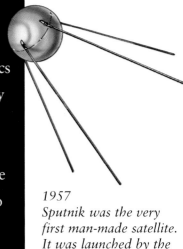

1957
Sputnik was the very first man-made satellite. It was launched by the former Soviet Union.

MAKE A RECEIVER DISH

A satellite dish collects weak signals and concentrates them to make a stronger signal. This model collects and concentrates light in the same way.

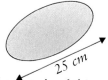

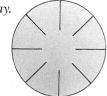

1 Cut a circle of thin card 25 cm in diameter. Glue it on to kitchen foil and cut round the edge.

2 Cut eight slots about 6 cm long from the edge of the circle towards the middle.

3 Bend up the segments to make a shallow dish. Use pieces of sticky tape to keep the dish in shape.

4 Point the dish towards a light or a window. Put a finger inside the dish, and you will see how it is lit up all round by the concentrated light that the dish collects.

MINI SATELLITE DISHES

There are two types of communications satellite. The first type relays signals between two ground stations, and is used to transmit telephone calls or television pictures between telephone or television networks. The second type can receive or transmit signals over a much wider area. This sort of satellite relays satellite television stations. The signals can be received with a mini satellite dish, about 30 cm across, although some need to be as wide as 80 cm, depending on where they are. Satellite television began in 1983. Recently, portable satellite dishes have become available, which can send telephone calls direct to a satellite. They are especially useful to news reporters working in parts of the world where there are no telephones. These systems can also send television pictures, as well as radio or computer information.

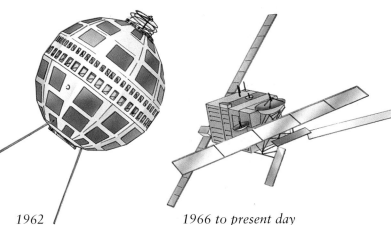

*1962
Telstar transmitted the first live television pictures across the Atlantic.*

*1966 to present day
Intelsat satellites give global coverage, allowing communication all over the world.*

*1981 to present day
The re-usable Space Shuttle takes satellites into space, where they are released into orbit. Astronauts aboard the Shuttle also recapture satellites to carry out repairs.*

COMPUTER COMMUNICATIONS

The first electronic computers were developed in the 1940s. They used hundreds of valves and were big enough to fill a room, but actually less powerful than a modern pocket calculator. The transistor, which is an electronic switch, was invented in 1948, and the integrated circuit, which allows complete electronic components to be fitted in a tiny silicon chip, was invented in 1958. Both these devices allowed computers to become much smaller and more powerful. By the end of the 1960s, many businesses had started using large computers called mainframes to store information (called data), such as their accounts and their customers' addresses. Before long, they were sending data between computers along special telephone lines. For example, a local bank could speedily get information about a customer's account from the bank's central computer.

A microprocessor is a tiny integrated circuit at the heart of every modern computer. After its invention in the early 1970s, computers quickly became cheaper. Today, most businesses use computers, and in large businesses, all the computers are connected so that they can exchange information. This is called a network.

THE PERSONAL COMPUTER
The first personal computer, the Altair 8800, was sold as a kit in 1975. Today, there are millions around the world. This computer is at the Save the Children Fund's office in a remote part of India.

A MODERN PERSONAL COMPUTER
A basic personal computer can be turned into a powerful communication machine by adding a modem, which allows computers to talk to each other and exchange information along normal telephone lines. Modem stands for modulator / demodulator.

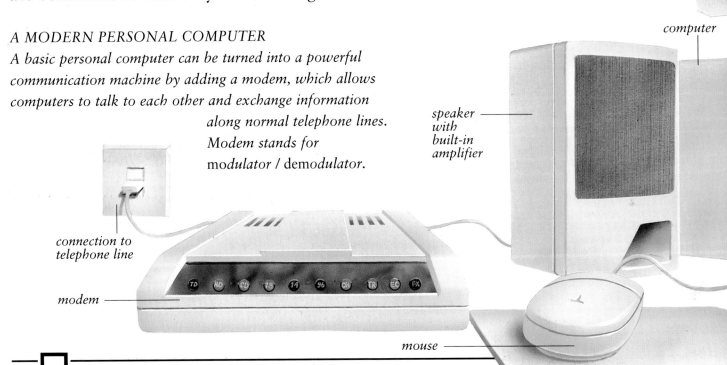

connection to telephone line

modem

speaker with built-in amplifier

computer

mouse

38

monitor

video camera

STANDARD CODES

Computers can only remember the numbers 0 and 1. To remember words, pictures, sounds, and so on, computers use codes of different combinations of 0s and 1s. When information is transferred between computers, each one must know the code, otherwise information gets muddled. The most common code for words is called ASCII (short for American Standard Code for Information Interchange). In ASCII, A= 65, B=66, C=67, and so on.

THE BACK OF A COMPUTER

external disk drive port   sound out port

printer port

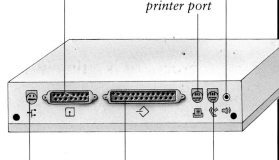

keyboard input   SCSI port   modem port

SCSI connector – a place to plug in extra pieces of equipment like scanners, disk drives and printers. It stands for Small Computer Systems Interface.

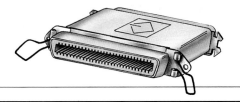

microphone   floppy disk drive

CD-ROM drive

keyboard

COMPUTER NETWORKS

A network is made when computers are linked together so that information can be sent from one to another. A network might have just two computers on it, or it might have many thousands. There are two types of network. The first type is a local area network (LAN for short). It consists of computers that are all in the same office, building or site. The data travels between the computers along electrical cables or optical fibres (see page 27). The second type of network is a wide area network (WAN for short). It consists of computers that are further apart and which are connected through the telephone network. A wide area network can include computers in different countries, or even on different sides of the world. You can send messages to another person on a network using electronic mail (e-mail for short). E-mail arrives in just a few seconds, and it's cheaper than the normal post.

LOCAL AREA NETWORK

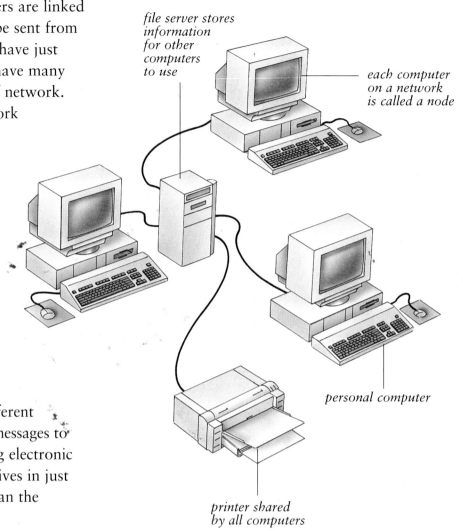

file server stores information for other computers to use

each computer on a network is called a node

personal computer

printer shared by all computers

ALL KINDS OF INFORMATION
You can get many different kinds of information and services on a personal computer with a modem to link it to the telephone network. Some services, such as home shopping, are called interactive services because you make choices on your screen about the information you want. Many of these services are also available on cable television channels.

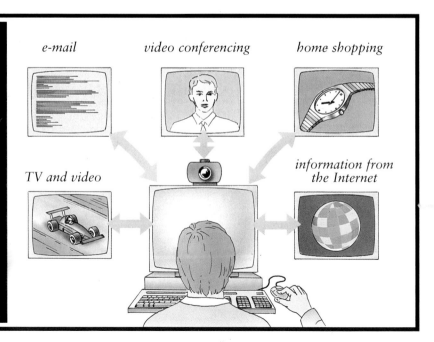

e-mail

video conferencing

home shopping

TV and video

information from the Internet

WIDE AREA NETWORK

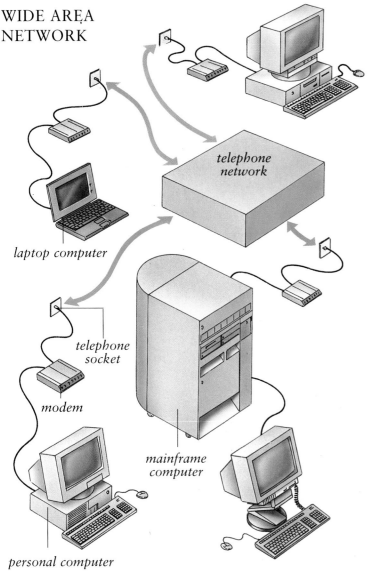

telephone network

laptop computer

telephone socket

modem

mainframe computer

personal computer

THE INTERNET

The Internet (or just the Net) is the largest computer network in the world. It links together hundreds of smaller computer networks at universities, government departments and other organisations throughout the world. The Internet started in the United States in 1984. Universities and research centres were linked to five powerful supercomputers via special telephone lines, so that researchers in one place could use computers that might be thousands of kilometres away. Researchers soon realised that they could send messages and information to each other over the network. Other organisations linked their computers to the Internet, and it began to grow rapidly. You can use the Internet for many different things, such as sending electronic mail (e-mail for short), finding all kinds of useful information, sending and receiving computer data, playing games, or simply talking to your friends. In early 1995, there were about 50,000 networks in the Internet, and up to 40 million people in over 150 countries were connected to it. Experts think that by the year 2005, there will be over 500 million people using the Internet.

ADVANCES IN REMOTE ACCESSING

Portable computers can be temporarily connected to a central computer through the telephone system, often from thousands of kilometres away. This is called remote accessing.

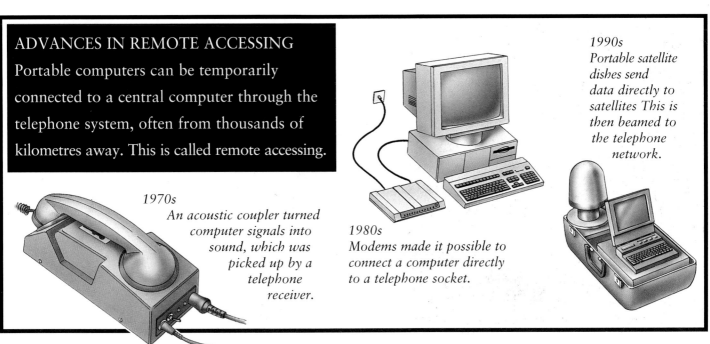

1970s
An acoustic coupler turned computer signals into sound, which was picked up by a telephone receiver.

1980s
Modems made it possible to connect a computer directly to a telephone socket.

1990s
Portable satellite dishes send data directly to satellites This is then beamed to the telephone network.

THE FUTURE

In the future, people will probably communicate in ways which would seem weird and wonderful to us – just as portable 'phones would seem amazing to Samuel Morse. Today, you might use a telephone attached to the telephone network to talk to friends, a television set with an aerial or satellite to watch programmes and videos, and a personal computer to send e-mail and get information over the Internet. In the future, you will probably need just one or two machines, such as teleputers and personal digital assistants, for all these things. There will be a huge growth in the amount of information and services you will be able to get at home or on a personal digital assistant, without ever having to visit a library or make 'phone calls. Experts think that by the year 2000, almost half the signals travelling through the world's telecommunications networks will be carrying information rather than speech. They call this the Information Superhighway.

A VIDEOPHONE
This videophone can transmit video images, speech, pictures and text using a small video camera on a personal computer. The quality is so good that deaf people can lip-read and sign to each other using the machine.

A VIRTUAL CONFERENCE
A virtual conference is a meeting in a virtual world created by a computer. It allows people thousands of kilometres apart to 'meet' and talk to each other as though they were in the same room. To go to a virtual meeting, you need to wear a special headset, which makes the pictures of the conference room look three-dimensional.

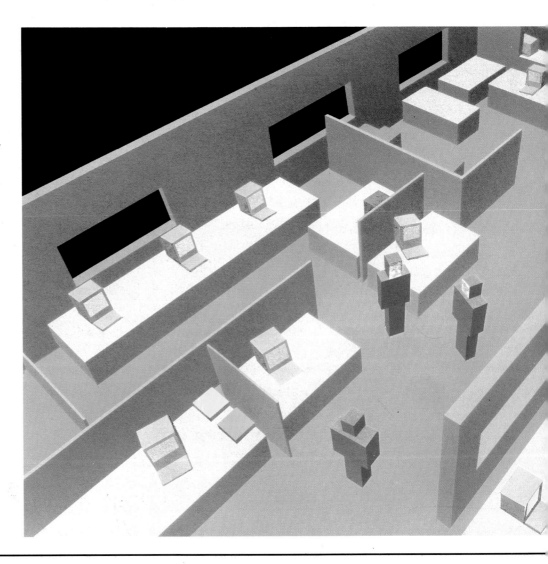

COMMUNICATIONS ON THE MOVE

Imagine an electronic digital diary with a notebook-sized screen and electronic pen, a mobile telephone, and a fax machine all combined and put in a box about the size of your hand. It's called a personal digital assistant (PDA for short), and it's what we will be carrying around with us in the near future. You can use a PDA as a normal telephone, to send and receive faxes and electronic mail. Eventually, PDAs will communicate with satellites so that you can communicate from anywhere in the world. And your PDA number won't include country or city codes – the intelligent, computerised telecommunications network will know where your PDA is all the time.

TELEPUTERS

A teleputer is a personal computer and television combined. It can do all the jobs of a computer, including receiving and sending electronic mail, computerised shopping, faxing, and also receive high-definition television (HDTV) pictures, which are wider and more detailed than standard pictures. Teleputers might become the communication and entertainment machine in every home.

THE SHAPE OF THINGS TO COME

Communication devices of the future may look completely different to the ones we know today. The electronics needed to make mobile telephones, fax machines, and so on, can be fitted into smaller and smaller spaces, and new ways of communicating with the machines themselves are being developed. Researchers at a British college have designed a mobile telephone in a glove, which is easier to carry than a normal telephone because it can be folded and put in your pocket. The mouthpiece is in the glove's palm. In the distant future, buttons may completely disappear, and you might be able to operate your personal digital assistant using your voice. For example, you might say 'Call Uncle Bob', and the machine would recognise the words, look up Uncle Bob's number and call it.

GLOSSARY

ACOUSTIC COUPLER A device which allows computers to send and receive information using a normal telephone receiver.

AERIAL A shaped piece of wire or a dish shape which transmits or receives radio signals.

AMPLIFY To make larger. An AMPLIFIER increases the strength of an electrical signal.

BINARY A way of writing down numbers using only 0s and 1s. Working from the right, each digit in binary code is worth double the one before (1, 2, 4, 8, 16, and so on). For example, 0001 = 1, 0011 = 2 + 1 = 3, 1101 = 8 + 4 + 1 = 13.

CHARACTER A letter or a sign or symbol meaning a word. Some languages, such as Japanese, use characters to represent whole words.

CIRCUIT An arrangement of wires and other electrical components through which electricity flows.

DATA Information stored or used by a computer.

EARTH An electrical connection to the ground. The ground can act as an extra wire in an electrical circuit.

EDIT Making corrections or changes to pieces of text.

ELECTROMAGNET A coil of wire which acts like a magnet when an electric current flows through the coil.

FLOPPY DISK A plastic disc covered in magnetic material which can store computer information.

FREQUENCY The number of times something happens every second. For example in radio waves the frequency is the number of waves which pass a point every second.

HDTV Short for high-definition television, which has much clearer pictures than normal television.

INTEGRATED CIRCUIT A single piece of a substance called silicon on which there is a complete electronic circuit, including all its components and all the connections between the components. Also called a SILICON CHIP.

MAINFRAME COMPUTER A large, powerful, high-speed computer which many people can use at the same time.

MICROPROCESSOR A complex integrated circuit which is at the heart of every computer.

MODULATION Combining a signal with a carrier signal so that it can be transmitted by radio or along telephone lines. Modulation is done by a MODULATOR at the transmitter and a DEMODULATOR takes away the carrier signal at the receiver.

PORT The name for a socket in a computer where information goes in or out.

REMOTE ACCESSING Temporarily connecting a portable computer to a network by telephone or satellite.

SCAN To divide a picture into thousands of tiny squares and work out the colour of each square so that the picture can be transmitted or stored on a computer.

SILICON CHIP see INTEGRATED CIRCUIT

STEREO A sound signal which contains information for two loudspeakers. This makes music from the speakers sound more realistic.

STYLUS A pointed writing implement or a pen.

TELEGRAPH A machine which sends letter and words along a wire as an electrical code.

TEXT Words that are written or printed.

TRANSISTOR An electrical device which can act as a switch or an amplifier.

VALVES Short for thermionic valve. An electronic device which could act as a switch or amplifier. Valves were contained in glass tubes a few centimetres long, and have now been replaced by transistors and other similar devices that are smaller.

VIDEO CONFERENCE A meeting where people in different places can see and talk to each other using video or computer links.

INDEX

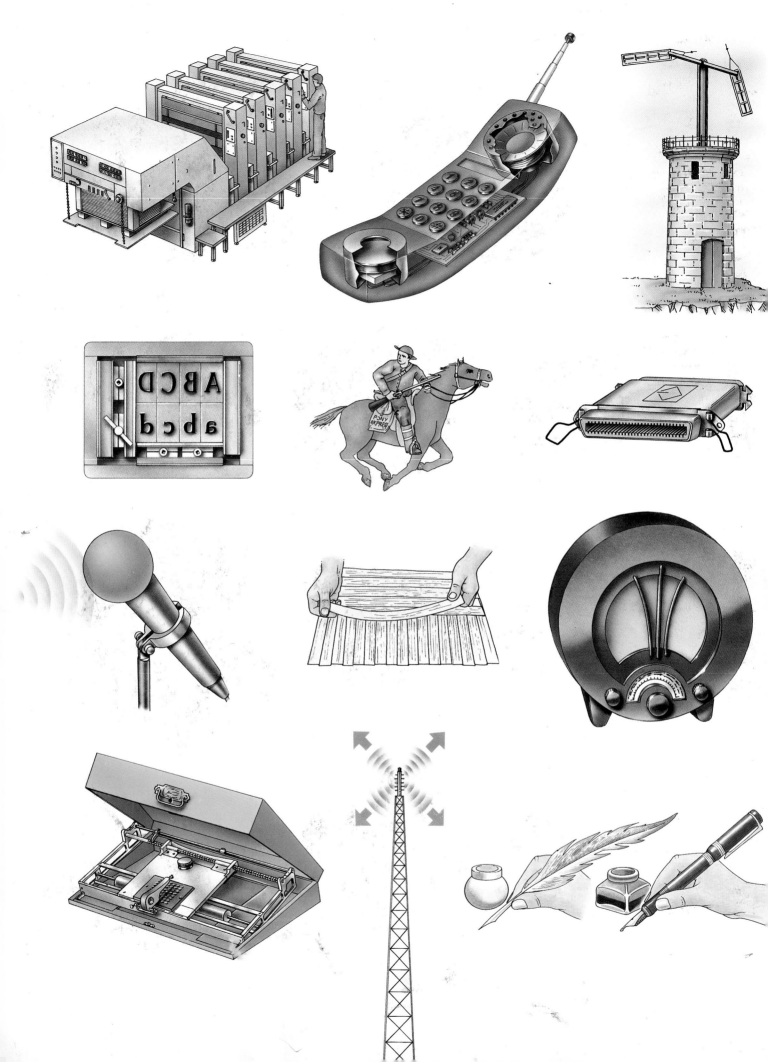